The Art of Good Food

PERFECT PIZZAS

JON HIGGINS

Illustrated by

PAUL COLLICUTT

CLB

The Art of Good Food

PERFECT PIZZAS

Designed and created by

THE BRIDGEWATER BOOK COMPANY LTD

Designer Sarah Stanley

Editor Donna Wood

Managing Editor Anna Clarkson

Illustrations Paul Collicut

Page make-up Heidi Green

CLB 4592

Colour separation by Sussex Repro, England

Printed and bound in Singapore by Tien Wah Press

ISBN 1-85833-555-8

Contents

Introduction

There can be no doubting the ever-increasing popularity of the pizza. What was once looked upon with a certain degree of suspicion is now a wholly accepted part of many people's diet. Supermarkets, delicatessens and fast-food chains are all looking for a 'slice' of the action, experimenting with varieties of ready prepared and ready cooked pizzas that achieve a high standard in presentation and taste. But what they are unable to achieve is the visual appeal and sheer individuality of the home-made pizza. We have all been told so many times that we eat initially with our eyes and I promise you that the first pizza you prepare from this collection of recipes will prove that there really is no better alternative to cooking them yourself.

If you have never prepared a pizza before, try to forget the prepacked and cellophane-covered varieties that vie for your attention on the supermarket shelves. No hand-prepared pizza will ever be or indeed should ever be perfectly circular, nor should they always be crammed to overflowing with a hotch-potch of unrelated toppings. Like many things in life, less often means more.

BASIC PIZZA DOUGH AND TOMATO SAUCE RECIPES

I have included two recipes for pizza dough in the book. One is a variation on the classic yeast-based dough, and as it is best to allow an hour for this to prove, you may prefer to use the quick pizza dough recipe if you are in a hurry. The quick pizza dough is easy to prepare, as the name implies, and can be used straightaway. It has a heavier, more biscuity texture. Of course, there is no reason why you cannot make whichever of the two bases you most prefer for any recipe and combine it with the topping of your choice.

Good home-made tomato sauce is of great importance to a successful pizza. Whilst in an ideal world we would all take great time and care skinning and deseeding Italian tomatoes, in reality we are often up against time. The recipe for tomato sauce contained in this book uses tomato purée. Although this may offend the purists, the simple addition of one or two extra ingredients to the sauce gives it a delicious slightly sweet flavour that is reminiscent of Italian tomatoes.

ANY SPECIAL EQUIPMENT?

There is no special equipment required to prepare and cook pizzas, although at some stage you may wish to purchase a perforated pizza pan, which enables the heat from the oven to get to the base and prevents it from becoming soggy. However this is not essential, as you can carefully slide the pizza off its baking sheet directly onto the oven shelf five minutes before the recommended cooking time is completed, and this will have the same effect.

By reading this introduction I hope you have realized that pizzas are far more rugged and versatile than you may have been led to believe. Providing the freshest cheese, meat, fish and herbs are used, even the most apprehensive cook can prepare a pizza, with guaranteed success.

Basic Pizza Dough

MAKES ONE 30CM/12-INCH PIZZA BASE

INGREDIENTS
225g/8oz strong plain flour
2.5ml/½tsp salt
5ml/1tsp easy blend dried yeast
15ml/1tbsp good quality olive oil
150ml/5fl oz warm water

Mix together the flour, salt and yeast and sift into a mixing bowl. Using your hand, make a well in the centre and add the olive oil and the warm water, gradually incorporating the flour until a sticky dough has formed.

Turn the dough out onto a floured work surface and knead well until it becomes smooth and elastic and all traces of stickiness have gone. To prevent a skin forming on the dough whilst it is proving, smear a little oil on the palms of your hands and lightly rub the surface.

Return the dough to a clean mixing bowl and leave somewhere warm for about an hour, or until it has doubled in size

When ready turn the dough out onto a floured surface and briefly 'knock back' to remove the air. The dough is now ready for rolling out to make a perfect pizza base.

Quick Pizza Dough

MAKES ONE 30CM/12-INCH PIZZA BASE

INGREDIENTS

225g/8oz strong plain flour
2.5ml/½tsp salt
2.5ml/½tsp sugar
50g/2oz lard
15ml/1tbsp olive oil
50ml/2fl oz milk

▌ Mix together the salt and flour and sift into a mixing bowl. Cut the fat into small pieces and, using your hands, rub into the flour until the mixture resembles fine breadcrumbs.

▌ Add the olive oil, milk and egg to the bowl and work together to form a soft dough.

▌ Turn the mixture onto the work surface and knead for a minute or two until smooth. This dough can be used immediately.

Tomato Sauce

SUFFICIENT FOR ONE 30CM/12-INCH PIZZA

INGREDIENTS

60ml/4tbsp olive oil
1 medium onion, finely chopped
30ml/2tbsp tomato purée
10ml/2tbsp clear honey
5ml/1tsp dried basil
5ml/1tsp dried oregano
1 bay leaf
salt and freshly ground black pepper

▌ Heat the olive oil in a saucepan and fry the onion until lightly browned.

▌ Add the remaining ingredients to the pan and bring to the boil. Lower the heat to a simmer and allow the contents of the pan to reduce until the sauce is glossy, thick and deep red in colour.

▌ Remove the bay leaf prior to use.

Ham & Asparagus Pizza Wheel

Asparagus gives this pizza a touch of luxury and a wonderfully fresh taste

INGREDIENTS

1 quantity Basic Pizza Dough *(page 10)*

12 asparagus spears, trimmed

1 quantity Tomato Sauce *(page 11)*

6 thin slices ham

50g/2oz Dolcelatte cheese, crumbled

50g/2oz Bel Paese cheese

60ml/4tbsp Mascarpone cheese

2tbsp milk

salt and freshly ground black pepper

Roll out the pizza dough to form a circle about 25cm/10 inches in diameter.

Place the dough on a lightly oiled baking sheet and prick all over with a fork. Allow to stand in a warm place while preparing the topping.

Bring a frying pan of water to the boil and add the asparagus. Cook for 4 minutes, then remove from the pan and plunge into cold water to prevent any further cooking.

Spread the tomato sauce over the pizza base.

Spread the ham slices out on a work surface. Sprinkle the Dolcelatte cheese along one side of each ham slice.

Roll up each slice of ham to form a cigar shape and arrange on top of the pizza like the spokes of a wheel.

Drain the asparagus well and arrange in between the rolls of ham.

Beat the Bel Paese until slightly softened, then beat in the Mascarpone and milk. Pour over the top of the pizza and season to taste with salt and freshly ground black pepper.

Place in a preheated oven at 200°C/400°F/Gas Mark 6 and bake for 20–25 minutes until the crust is golden and the cheese mixture lightly browned.

TIME: Preparation takes about 15 minutes. Cooking takes approximately 25 minutes.

Four Seasons Pizza

MAKES ONE 25CM/10-INCH PIZZA

A *classic pizza with no less than four different toppings*

INGREDIENTS

1 quantity Basic Pizza Dough *(page 10)*

60ml/4tbsp passata

1ST QUARTER

olive oil

50g/2oz mushrooms, sliced

2ND QUARTER

1 slice Parma ham, cut into strips

2 pitted black olives, chopped

25g/1oz mozzarella cheese, grated

3RD QUARTER

4 canned artichoke hearts, sliced

1 clove garlic, chopped

2.5ml/½tsp chopped fresh oregano

olive oil

4TH QUARTER

25g/1oz smoked mozzarella cheese, grated

75g/3oz mixed shellfish

5ml/1tsp chopped fresh parsley

olive oil

salt and freshly ground black pepper

▌ Roll out the pizza dough to form a circle about 25cm/10 inches in diameter.

▌ Place the dough on a lightly oiled baking sheet and prick all over with a fork.

▌ Spread with the passata and gently mark into quarters. Allow to stand in a warm place while preparing the topping.

▌ Heat 2 tbsp olive oil in a small pan and sauté the mushrooms for 4 minutes or until just softened. Arrange on one section of the pizza.

▌ Mix the Parma ham with the olives. Pile onto another section of the pizza. Sprinkle the mozzarella cheese on top.

▌ Arrange the artichokes on the third section of the pizza. Mix together the garlic and oregano and scatter on top. Drizzle with a little olive oil.

▌ Scatter the smoked cheese on the final section of the pizza and arrange the shellfish on top. Sprinkle with parsley and drizzle with a little olive oil.

▌ Season the whole pizza with salt and pepper.

▌ Bake in a preheated oven at 220°C/425°F/Gas Mark 7 for 15 minutes, then reduce the heat to 190°C/375°F/Gas Mark 5 and bake for a further 20 minutes until the base is cooked and golden. Serve immediately.

TIME: Preparation takes about 20 minutes. Cooking takes approximately 35 minutes.

Spicy Lamb Pizza

MAKES ONE 23CM/9-INCH PIZZA

If *you marinate the meat overnight,*
this pizza will be very quick to prepare on the day of eating

INGREDIENTS

45ml/3tbsp dark soy sauce

5ml/1tsp Worcestershire sauce

10ml/2tsp sherry vinegar

1 clove garlic, crushed

1/2 small onion, grated or very finely chopped

2.5ml/1/4tsp ground cumin

2.5ml/1/4tsp ground coriander

1cm/1/2inch piece root ginger, peeled and grated

175g/6oz lean lamb, sliced into strips

1 quantity Quick Pizza Dough *(page 11)*

1 quantity Tomato Sauce *(page 11)*

50g/2oz Cheddar cheese, grated

45ml/3tbsp freshly grated Parmesan cheese

❚ Put the soy and Worcestershire sauce, the vinegar, garlic, onion, cumin, coriander and ginger in a shallow dish and stir until well combined.

❚ Add the meat, toss until well coated and marinate overnight.

❚ The following day prepare the pizza dough. Roll it out to form a circle about 23cm/9 inches in diameter.

❚ Place the dough on a lightly oiled baking sheet and prick all over with a fork.

❚ Spread the tomato sauce over the pizza base.

❚ Remove the meat from the marinade with a slotted spoon and scatter over the pizza.

❚ Mix together the two cheeses and sprinkle over the top of the pizza.

❚ Bake in a preheated oven at 240°C/475°F/Gas Mark 9 for 20 minutes or until the pizza has risen and turned golden brown and the meat is just cooked.

TIME: Preparation takes about 10 minutes, plus marinating.

Cooking takes approximately 20 minutes.

15

Chicken Pizza with Thai Spices

MAKES ONE 23CM/9-INCH PIZZA

Spicy chicken and sweet yellow peppers top this Oriental-style pizza

INGREDIENTS

1 quantity Quick Pizza Dough *(page 11)*

30ml/2tbsp sunflower oil

½ yellow pepper, seeded and chopped

25g/1oz butter

50g/2oz button mushrooms

10ml/2tsp Thai 7-spice

1 chicken breast, skinned, boned and cut into strips

bunch of spring onions, cut into 2.5cm/
1inch lengths

1 quantity Tomato Sauce *(page 11)*

3 processed cheese slices, cut into strips

coriander sprigs, to garnish

▌Roll out the pizza dough to form a circle about 23cm/9 inches in diameter.

▌Place the dough on a lightly oiled baking sheet and prick all over with a fork.

▌Bake in a preheated oven at 200°C/400°F/ Gas Mark 6 for 15 minutes or until golden-brown. Reduce the heat to 180°C/350°F/Gas Mark 4.

▌Meanwhile, heat the oil in a frying pan and fry the pepper for 5 minutes until just beginning to soften. Remove with a slotted spoon and set aside.

▌Add the butter and stir until melted, sauté the mushrooms for 2 minutes, remove and set aside.

▌Add the Thai 7-spice and cook over a low heat for 1 minute.

▌Stir in the chicken and toss until well coated, then increase the heat and cook until the chicken begins to brown.

▌Return the mushrooms to the pan, add the spring onions, toss together, then remove from the heat.

▌Spread the tomato sauce over the part-cooked pizza base. Sprinkle with half the chopped pepper. Spread the chicken mixture over the pizza.

▌Sprinkle with the remaining chopped pepper and the cheese.

▌Return to the oven and bake for 10–15 minutes until the base is cooked and golden.

▌Serve garnished with fresh coriander.

TIME: Preparation takes about 25 minutes.

Cooking takes approximately 30 minutes.

17

Pizza with Warm Chicken Livers

MAKES ONE 30CM/12-INCH PIZZA

Chicken livers make a deliciously rich pizza topping

INGREDIENTS

15ml/1tbsp sesame seeds

1 quantity Quick Pizza Dough *(page 11)*

2 medium red onions, thinly sliced

30ml/2tbsp olive oil

½ quantity Tomato Sauce *(page 11)*

450g/1lb chicken livers

salt and freshly ground black pepper

25g/1oz flour

75g/3oz butter

50ml/2fl oz Madeira or sweet sherry

sage leaves, to garnish (optional)

Lightly toast the sesame seeds under a preheated grill. Allow them to cool then knead them into the prepared pizza dough and roll it out 30cm/12 inches in diameter.

Place the prepared base on a lightly greased pizza pan and set to one side.

Fry the onions in the olive oil until they soften and begin to brown a little, then using a slotted spoon remove them from the pan and leave to drain on absorbent kitchen paper. Spread the prepared base evenly with the tomato sauce and arrange the onions on top, brush the edges of the pizza base with oil and place in a preheated oven 240°C/475°F/Gas Mark 9 for 20 minutes.

Whilst the base is cooking, rinse the chicken livers under cold running water and dry them. Carefully look over the livers and cut away any white or discoloured areas with a sharp knife.

If the livers are quite large cut them to an even size; this will make a far more attractive pizza.

Season the prepared livers with plenty of salt and fresh black pepper and toss them in the flour so they all receive a good coating. Melt the butter in a frying pan and fry the livers briefly on both sides for a couple of minutes until lightly browned, but still pink inside.

Remove the livers from the pan and arrange them over the cooked base. Reheat the juices in the frying pan and add the Madeira or sherry, reduce briefly before spooning a little over the finished pizza.

Garnish with a few sage leaves, if liked and serve immediately.

TIME: Preparation takes about 25 minutes. Cooking takes approximately 25 minutes.

18

Pizza with Garlic Sausage

MAKES ONE 25CM/10-INCH PIZZA

A *colourful and very tasty pizza*

INGREDIENTS

1 quantity Basic Pizza Dough *(page 10)*

1 quantity Tomato Sauce *(page 11)*

30ml/2tbsp olive oil

$^{1}/_{2}$ red pepper, seeded and cut into rings

$^{1}/_{2}$ green pepper, seeded and cut into rings

$^{1}/_{2}$ yellow pepper, seeded and cut into rings

125g/4oz garlic sausage, sliced

125g/4oz mozzarella cheese, grated

6 pitted black olives, sliced

▌Roll out the pizza dough to form a circle about 25cm/10 inches in diameter.

▌Place the dough on a lightly oiled baking sheet and prick all over with a fork.

▌Spread the pizza base with the tomato sauce and allow to stand in a warm place while preparing the topping.

▌Heat the oil in a large frying pan and fry the peppers for 5 minutes, stirring constantly until just softened.

▌Make a ring of garlic sausage around the outside of the pizza. Add another ring of peppers, alternating the colours.

▌Place the remaining rings in the centre of the pizza.

▌Sprinkle with cheese and top with the olives.

▌Bake in a preheated oven at 200°C/400°F/ Gas Mark 6 for 25–30 minutes or until the base is cooked and golden.

TIME: *Preparation takes about 10 minutes.*
Cooking takes approximately 40 minutes.

19

Calzone

MAKES 4 CALZONE

This is a folded pizza from Naples and is
ideal for picnics

INGREDIENTS
1 quantity Basic Pizza Dough *(page 10)*
4 slices Parma ham, cut into strips
125g/4oz Bel Paese cheese, cut into small pieces
8 anchovy fillets
salt and freshly ground black pepper
olive oil for brushing

▌Divide the pizza dough into four. Roll out each piece
to form a circle about 18cm/7-inch in diameter.
▌Place a quarter of the ham, cheese and 2 anchovy
fillets on one side of each round of dough. Season with
salt and pepper.
▌Dampen the edges with a little water and fold the
dough over to enclose the filling. Pinch the edges
together well to seal and brush with a little olive oil.
▌Place on a lightly oiled baking sheet and bake in a
preheated oven at 200°C/400°F/Gas Mark 6 for about
20 minutes or until the dough is crisp and golden. Serve
hot or cold.

TIME: *Preparation takes about 10 minutes.*
Cooking takes approximately 20 minutes.

French Bread Pizza

SERVES 4

French bread pizzas make a delicious snack
and are also ideal for parties

INGREDIENTS
1 small French stick
90ml/6tbsp tomato pizza or pasta sauce
Selection of: ham, pepperoni, salami, diced bacon,
sliced mushrooms, sweetcorn, diced peppers, pineapple,
chopped tomatoes, prawns
50g/2oz mozzarella cheese, grated
50g/2oz Cheddar cheese, grated
chopped fresh oregano

▌Cut the French stick in half lengthways and in half
again to form four bases.
▌Toast the cut sides under a preheated grill until
just browned.
▌Spread the bases with pizza or pasta sauce and top with
a selection of your choice.
▌Mix together the two cheeses and the oregano, and
sprinkle over the pizza.
▌Place under the grill until the cheese melts and the
toppings are heated through. Serve at once.

TIME: *Preparation takes about 10 minutes.*
Cooking takes approximately 5 minutes.

20

Game & Tarragon Pizza

MAKES ONE 30CM/12-INCH PIZZA

Rabbit meat is full of flavour. It deserves to be more popular

INGREDIENTS

1 quantity Quick Pizza Dough *(page 11)*
125ml/4fl oz red wine
1 quantity Tomato Sauce *(page 11)*
450g/1lb boned rabbit meat
45ml/3tbsp olive oil
30ml/2tbsp finely chopped tarragon
salt and freshly ground black pepper

Roll out the pizza dough and place on a lightly oiled pizza pan.

Mix together the red wine and tomato sauce and pour into a saucepan. Bring to the boil then lower the heat and allow the liquid to reduce to a very thick sauce. Spread the sauce evenly over the pizza base to within 2.5cm/1 inch of the edge.

Dice the rabbit meat into small pieces, approximately 5mm/¼ inch in size. Heat 30ml/2tbsp of the olive oil in a frying pan and lightly fry the diced rabbit until golden.

Using a slotted spoon, remove the rabbit from the pan and spread evenly over the tomato sauce, sprinkle over chopped tarragon and season with salt and plenty of black pepper.

Drizzle the remaining 15ml/1tbsp olive oil over the top of the pizza and place in a preheated oven 240°C/475°F/Gas Mark 9 for 15–20 minutes until well risen with a crisp, golden edge.

This rich pizza is complemented by a glass of full-bodied red wine.

TIME: *Preparation takes about 25 minutes. Cooking takes approximately 20 minutes.*

English Triple Banger Pizza

These sausages work well together, but you can use others if you wish

INGREDIENTS

1 quantity Basic Pizza Dough *(page 10)*

1 quantity Tomato Sauce *(page 11)*

50g/2oz black pudding

50g/2oz Cumberland sausage

50g/2oz spicy English sausage

1 medium onion, thinly sliced in rings

olive oil

125g/4oz button mushrooms, sliced

75g/3oz Cheddar cheese, grated

Roll out the pizza dough into a rectangular shape of roughly 25cm x 30cm/10 x 12 inches and place on a lightly oiled baking sheet. Spread with the tomato sauce and set to one side.

Slice the black pudding thinly and place on a grill pan with the Cumberland sausage and spicy English sausage. (These should be pricked a few times with a fork to prevent their skins from bursting whilst cooking.)

Place under a preheated grill and cook until the sausages have browned evenly all over and the black pudding is crisp.

Fry the onion rings in 30ml/2tbsp olive oil until soft and golden. Add the sliced button mushrooms and briefly toss together with the onion so they absorb the olive oil, then remove the pan from the heat and spread the mixture over the pizza base.

Slice the cooked sausages thinly and evenly distribute them over the top of the pizza along with the black pudding and finish with a good sprinkling of grated Cheddar.

Place the pizza in a preheated oven 240°C/475°F/Gas Mark 9 for 15 minutes or until the cheese has melted into the sausage and the base is well risen and browned.

TIME: *Preparation takes about 30 minutes. Cooking takes approximately 15 minutes.*

Club Sandwich Pizza

MAKES TWO *13CM/5-INCH* SANDWICHES

Yௌou will probably want to share this pizza with a friend – it's very filling

INGREDIENTS

2 quantities Quick Pizza Dough *(page 11)*

olive oil

5ml/1tsp tomato purée

125ml/4fl oz mayonnaise

225g/8oz cooked peeled prawns

4 slices of rare roast beef

10ml/2 tsp creamed horseradish sauce

225g/8oz chicken breast, chopped

2 tomatoes, seeded and chopped

lettuce leaves, to garnish

Roll out the pizza dough thinly and cut eight 13cm/5 inch circles from it using an upturned basin or similar as a cutter.

Place the dough circles onto lightly oiled baking sheets and brush over with a little olive oil. Place in a preheated oven 240°C/475°F/Gas Mark 9 for 15–20 minutes until risen and nicely browned. Remove from the oven and transfer to a cooling rack.

To prepare the fillings, beat the tomato purée into 75ml/3fl oz of the mayonnaise and combine with the prawns. Spread the prawn mayonnaise over 2 of the pizza bases and sandwich with another 2 bases.

Next, lay 2 slices of roast beef on top of the sandwiches and spread each with a teaspoon of horseradish sauce, again cover with a pizza base.

For the final layer, combine the chicken breast, chopped tomato flesh and the remaining mayonnaise and spread over the sandwich, topping with the last 2 pizza circles.

Using a sharp knife, cut the sandwiches in half and to aid presentation push a wooden skewer through each to keep the layers together. Garnish with fresh lettuce leaves and serve.

TIME: *Preparation takes about 15 minutes.*
Cooking takes approximately 15 minutes.

25

*P*izzette

MAKES 8 MINI PIZZAS

*M*ini pizzas are great for children and ideal at parties

INGREDIENTS

1 quantity Basic Pizza Dough *(page 10)*

1 quantity Tomato Sauce *(page 11)*

small bunch of spring onions, sliced

15ml/1tbsp olive oil

50g/2oz mushrooms, sliced

2 gherkins, sliced

4 slices salami, cut into strips

50g/2oz Red Leicester cheese, grated

50g/2oz mozzarella cheese, grated

chopped fresh oregano

salt and freshly ground black pepper

▌Divide the pizza dough into 8 smooth balls.

▌Roll out each ball to form a circle about 10cm/4 inches in diameter.

▌Place on a lightly oiled baking sheet and prick all over with a fork.

▌Spread the tomato sauce over each pizza base and allow to stand in a warm place while preparing the rest of the topping.

▌Scatter a few slices of spring onion onto each pizza.

▌Heat the oil in a small saucepan and sauté the mushrooms for 2 minutes until just softened. Arrange over 4 of the pizza bases.

▌Arrange the gherkins and salami on the remaining pizza bases.

▌Mix together the cheeses, oregano and seasoning and divide between the 8 pizzas.

▌Bake in a preheated oven at 200°C/400°F/Gas Mark 6 for 20–25 minutes or until the bases are cooked and golden.

TIME: *Preparation takes about 20 minutes.*
Cooking takes approximately 25 minutes.

Spinach & Ham Pizza

MAKES ONE 23CM/9-INCH PIZZA

A *colourful and unusual pizza topping which is ideal for parties*

INGREDIENTS

1 quantity Quick Pizza Dough *(page 11)*

30ml/2tbsp sunflower oil

1 onion, chopped

1 clove garlic, crushed

225g/8oz frozen spinach, chopped

salt and freshly ground black pepper

pinch of freshly grated nutmeg

1 quantity Tomato Sauce *(page 11)*

30ml/2tbsp pine nuts

50g/2oz Parma ham

75g/3oz mozzarella cheese, sliced

olive oil

▌ Roll out the pizza dough to form a circle about 23cm/9 inches in diameter.

▌ Place the dough on a lightly oiled baking sheet and prick all over with a fork.

▌ Bake in a preheated oven at 200°C/400°F/Gas Mark 6 for 15 minutes or until golden. Reduce the heat to 180°C/350°F/Gas Mark 4.

▌ Heat the oil in a saucepan and fry the onion for 4 minutes until beginning to soften.

▌ Add the garlic and fry for 1 minute.

▌ Reduce the heat and add the frozen spinach. Cook over a very low heat until it has thawed, stirring occasionally. Increase the heat and boil off any liquid. Season with salt, pepper and nutmeg.

▌ Spread the tomato sauce over the part-cooked pizza base, then spoon over the spinach mixture. Scatter half the pine nuts on top of the spinach.

▌ Crinkle up the Parma ham and arrange on top of the pizza along with the cheese.

▌ Brush the ham with a little extra oil and top with the remaining pine nuts.

▌ Return to the oven and bake for 10–15 minutes until the cheese has melted.

TIME: *Preparation takes about 20 minutes.*
Cooking takes approximately 40 minutes.

27

Pizza Pronto

MAKES ONE 25CM/10-INCH PIZZA

A ready-made pizza base is great if you want a really quick snack

INGREDIENTS

1 x 25cm/10-inch ready-made pizza base

225g/8fl oz jar passata

125g/4oz jar marinated peppers

125g/4oz fresh mushrooms, sliced

25g/1oz snack salami, cut into chunks (optional)

125g/4oz mozzarella cheese, grated

▌Place the pizza base on a lightly oiled baking sheet and spread with the passata.

▌Arrange the peppers, mushrooms and salami, if using, over the sauce and sprinkle with the grated cheese.

▌Bake in a preheated oven at 240°C/475°F/Gas Mark 7 for 10–15 minutes

TIME: *Preparation takes about 5 minutes. Cooking takes approximately 15 minutes.*

Pizza Tropicana

MAKES ONE 23CM/9-INCH PIZZA

A popular pizza which is very simple to prepare

INGREDIENTS

1 quantity Quick Pizza Dough *(page 11)*

1 quantity Tomato Sauce *(page 11)*

pinch of ground allspice

2 thick slices ham, cut into squares

50g/2oz canned pineapple chunks, drained weight

salt and freshly ground black pepper

chopped fresh oregano

125g/4oz mozzarella cheese, grated

▌Roll out the pizza dough to form a circle about 23cm/9 inches in diameter.

▌Place the dough on a lightly oiled baking sheet and prick all over with a fork.

▌Spread the tomato sauce over the pizza dough and sprinkle with a generous pinch of allspice.

▌Arrange the ham and pineapple on top.

▌Season with salt and pepper, then sprinkle with fresh oregano and grated cheese.

▌Bake in a preheated oven at 190°C/375°F/Gas Mark 5 for 35–40 minutes or until the base is cooked.

TIME: *Preparation takes about 10 minutes. Cooking takes approximately 40 minutes.*

28

American-style Spicy Beef Pizza

MAKES ONE 25CM/10-INCH PIZZA

Omit the chilli to make this a perfect pizza for kids

INGREDIENTS

1 quantity Basic Pizza Dough *(page 10)*

175g/6oz lean minced beef

¹/₂ small onion, very finely chopped

1 clove garlic, crushed

5ml/1tsp ground allspice

5ml/1tsp ground chilli

olive oil, for frying

¹/₂ red pepper, seeded and chopped

¹/₂ green pepper, seeded and chopped

1 quantity Tomato Sauce *(page 11)*

75g/3oz Cheddar cheese, grated

▌Roll the pizza dough out to form a circle about 25cm/10 inches in diameter.

▌Place the dough on a lightly oiled baking sheet, and prick all over with a fork. Allow to stand in a warm place while preparing the topping.

▌Put the beef, onion, garlic, allspice and chilli in a mixing bowl and mix together with your hands until well combined.

▌Shape the mixture into 18 balls, pressing it together well as you do so.

▌Shallow fry in olive oil for about 5 minutes until browned on all sides.

▌Place the meat balls on top of the pizza base and scatter with the chopped peppers.

▌Carefully spoon tomato sauce over the pizza.

▌Sprinkle with grated cheese and bake in a preheated oven at 240°C/475°F/Gas Mark 9 for 20–25 minutes or until the base is well risen and golden.

TIME: *Preparation takes about 20 minutes. Cooking takes approximately 25 minutes.*

Deep Pan Christmas Pizza

MAKES ONE 25CM/10-INCH PIZZA

Here's proof that you don't have to make a curry with the Christmas leftovers

INGREDIENTS

1 quantity Quick Pizza Dough *(page 11)*

225g/8oz fresh or frozen cranberries

50g/2oz fresh or frozen blueberries

15ml/1tbsp granulated sugar

450g/1lb turkey breast, chopped

175g/6oz sage and onion stuffing, prepared

olive oil

fresh sage, to garnish (optional)

For the best results use a shallow, loose-bottomed flan tin to make this pizza. Lightly oil the base to prevent sticking.

Roll the dough out into a circle roughly 2.5cm/1inch larger than the tin itself and line it, making sure you press the dough well into the corners and up the sides. Trim away any excess with a knife.

Prick the base of the pizza all over with a fork, lightly brush with olive oil and place in a preheated oven 240°C/475°F/Gas Mark 9 for 5 minutes to seal the pastry.

Place the cranberries and blueberries in a saucepan along with the sugar and a tiny drop of water to prevent burning, and simmer gently until the fruit softens to a pulp.

Spread a thin layer of the cranberry sauce over the base of the pizza.

In a mixing bowl, gently stir together the chopped turkey and prepared stuffing and spread it over the pizza.

Brush the surface with a little olive oil and return the finished pizza to the oven for 15–20 minutes or until the crust has browned nicely and the filling is hot.

Garnish with a few torn sage leaves, if liked, and serve immediately.

TIME: *Preparation takes about 15 minutes. Cooking takes approximately 25 minutes.*

Parma Ham & Fresh Fig Pizza

MAKES ONE 30CM/12-INCH PIZZA

The *flavour of fresh figs is truly exotic*

INGREDIENTS

1 quantity Quick Pizza Dough *(page 11)*

1 quantity Tomato Sauce *(page 11)*

8 slices Parma ham

2 fresh ripe figs

175g/6oz mozzarella cheese, grated

olive oil

fresh basil leaves, to garnish

▌ Roll out the pizza dough and place on a pizza pan. Spread the tomato sauce evenly over the surface to within 1mm/½inch of the edge.

▌ Arrange the Parma ham on top and brush the exposed rim of the pizza with olive oil. Place in a preheated oven at 240°C/475°F/Gas Mark 9.

▌ Prepare the figs by thinly slicing downwards through the flesh.

▌ After approximately 10 minutes remove the pizza from the oven and arrange the slices of fig over the pizza and sprinkle liberally with grated mozzarella cheese.

▌ Drizzle a little olive oil over the top and return the pizza to the oven for a further 10 minutes or until the cheese has melted and the crust is crisp and golden.

▌ Roughly tear a few basil leaves for garnish and serve straightaway.

TIME: *Preparation takes about 15 minutes. Cooking takes approximately 20 minutes.*

33

Meat Feast

If the meat begins to dry out, cover the pizza with a loose tent of foil

INGREDIENTS
1 quantity Basic Pizza Dough *(page 10)*
1 quantity Tomato Sauce *(page 11)*
50g/2oz mushrooms, sliced
125g/4oz selection of sliced meats, such as salami,
pepperoni, garlic sausage, ham or pastrami
50g/2oz mozzarella cheese, grated
olive oil
salt and freshly ground black pepper

▌Roll out the pizza dough to form a circle about 25cm/10 inches in diameter.

▌Place the dough on a lightly oiled baking sheet and prick all over with a fork. Allow to stand in a warm place for 15 minutes.

▌Spread the tomato sauce over the pizza base and scatter the mushrooms on top.

▌Cut any large slices of meat into smaller pieces and arrange on the pizza. Sprinkle with grated cheese.

▌Drizzle with olive oil and season with salt and pepper.

▌Bake in a preheated oven at 200°C/400°F/Gas Mark 6 for 15 minutes, then reduce the heat to 190°C/375°F/ Gas Mark 5 and bake for a further 20 minutes or until the base is cooked and golden.

TIME: *Preparation takes about 10 minutes. Cooking takes approximately 30 minutes.*

Mascarpone Cheese & Pastrami Pizza

A mouthwatering combination!

INGREDIENTS
1 quantity Quick Pizza Dough *(page 10)*
225g/8oz Mascarpone cheese
10ml/2tsp made-up English mustard
2 cloves garlic, crushed
salt and freshly ground black pepper
8 slices pastrami
8 thin slices of tomato
a few black olives, sliced
olive oil

▌Roll out the dough and place on a lightly oiled pizza pan. Mix together the Mascarpone cheese, English mustard and garlic and season well.

▌Spread the cheese mixture over the pizza base to within 15mm/¹/₂inch of the edge.

▌Arrange the pastrami and tomato slices alternately around the pizza and sprinkle with the sliced olives. Season and drizzle over a little olive oil.

▌Place in a preheated oven 240°C/475°F/Gas Mark 9 for 15–20 minutes until the base is golden brown and the topping is heated through. Serve immediately.

TIME: *Preparation takes about 10 minutes. Cooking takes approximately 20 minutes.*

American Hot Pizza

MAKES ONE 25CM/10-INCH PIZZA

Hot and spicy!

INGREDIENTS

1 quantity Basic Pizza Dough *(page 10)*

50g/2oz butter

125g/4oz mushrooms, sliced

1 quantity Tomato Sauce *(page 11)*

2 green chillies, seeded and sliced into rings

50g/2oz pepperoni, sliced

125g/4oz mozzarella cheese, sliced

▌ Roll out the pizza dough to form a circle about 25cm/10 inches in diameter.

▌ Place the dough on a lightly oiled baking sheet and prick all over with a fork. Allow to stand in a warm place while preparing the topping.

▌ Melt the butter in a small saucepan and sauté the mushrooms for 2–3 minutes or until softened.

▌ Spread the tomato sauce over the pizza base, then cover with the sautéed mushrooms.

▌ Scatter half the chillies over the mushrooms, then top with a layer of pepperoni.

▌ Lay the cheese on top and scatter with the remaining chillies.

▌ Bake in a preheated oven at 200°C/400°F/Gas Mark 6 for 25–30 minutes or until the base is cooked and golden and the cheese has melted.

TIME: *Preparation takes about 20 minutes. Cooking takes approximately 30 minutes.*

36

Salt Beef & Horseradish Pizza

MAKES ONE 30CM/12-INCH PIZZA

This pizza combines several strong flavours to good effect

INGREDIENTS

1 quantity Basic Pizza Dough *(page 10)*

olive oil

50ml/2fl oz cream of horseradish sauce

225g/8oz mature Cheddar cheese, grated

10ml/2tsp prepared English mustard

8 thin slices salt beef

freshly ground black pepper

chopped watercress, to garnish

▌Roll out the pizza dough and place on a lightly oiled pizza pan. Brush the surface with a little olive oil.

▌In a bowl mix together the horseradish sauce, grated Cheddar cheese and English mustard. Spread the mixture evenly over the top of the pizza, leaving a 2.5cm/1inch gap around the edge.

▌Arrange the salt beef slices ranging from the centre of the pizza like the spokes of a wheel, then grind fresh black pepper over the top.

▌Place in a preheated oven 240°C/475°F/Gas Mark 9 for 15–20 minutes until the dough has risen and the cheese mixture is bubbling.

▌Remove the pizza from the oven and garnish with chopped watercress before serving.

TIME: *Preparation takes about 10 minutes. Cooking takes approximately 20 minutes.*

37

New Cuban Pizza

MAKES ONE 30CM/12-INCH PIZZA

Combining exotic fresh fish and ripe fruit will enliven the most jaded of palates

INGREDIENTS

175g/6oz fresh tuna

175g/6oz fresh red snapper

juice of 2 limes

30ml/2tbsp chopped shallots

salt and freshly ground black pepper

1 quantity Basic Pizza Dough *(page 10)*

1 quantity Tomato Sauce *(page 11)*

1 small ripe mango, peeled and cut into

1cm/$^1/_2$ inch dice

▌ Carefully remove any skin and bone from the fish and cut it into chunks approximately 2.5cm/1inch in size. Place the prepared fish in a shallow bowl.

▌ Mix together the lime juice, chopped shallots and plenty of seasoning and pour over the fish. Cover and set aside to marinate for a couple of hours, stirring occasionally to combine the flavours.

▌ When the fish has had sufficient time to marinate, roll the pizza dough out on a lightly floured surface and place on an oiled pizza pan.

▌ Spread the tomato sauce over the dough to within 1cm/$^1/_2$inch of the edge and begin cooking in a preheated oven 240°C/475°F/Gas Mark 9 for 10 minutes.

▌ Drain off the marinade and arrange the fish chunks over the partly cooked pizza base. Return to the oven for a further 10 minutes until the fish has just cooked and the pizza dough is crisp and well risen.

▌ Scatter the diced mango over the pizza and place in the oven for a few minutes to warm through. Serve immediately.

TIME: *Preparation takes about 15 minutes, plus marinating.*

Cooking takes approximately 25 minutes.

38

Tasty Tuna Pizza

A *substantial pizza using ingredients from several European countries*

INGREDIENTS

1 quantity Basic Pizza Dough *(page 10)*

2 beef tomatoes, sliced

1 red onion, sliced

175g/6oz can tuna, drained

1 hard boiled egg, cut into wedges

125g/4oz Feta cheese, cubed

8 pitted black olives

45ml/3tbsp olive oil

15ml/1tbsp white wine vinegar

salt and freshly ground black pepper

fresh basil leaves, to garnish

▌Roll out the pizza dough to form a circle about 25cm/10 inches in diameter.

▌Place the dough on a lightly oiled baking sheet and prick all over with a fork. Allow to stand in a warm place for 15 minutes.

▌Arrange the tomato slices and onion on top of the pizza base.

▌Bake in a preheated oven at 200°C/400°F/Gas Mark 6 for 10 minutes.

▌Break the tuna into chunks and place on top of the pizza.

▌Arrange the egg wedges on the pizza along with the Feta cheese and olives.

▌Whisk together the oil, vinegar and seasoning with a fork and sprinkle over the pizza.

▌Bake for 15–20 minutes or until the base is cooked and golden.

▌Top with fresh basil leaves, to garnish.

TIME: *Preparation takes about 30 minutes. Cooking takes approximately 30 minutes.*

40

Sweet Pepper & Whitebait Star

A *pizza to impress your dinner guests*

INGREDIENTS

2 quantities Quick Pizza Dough *(page 11)*

30ml/2tbsp olive oil

1 green and 1 yellow pepper seeded and sliced into rings

1 quantity Tomato Sauce *(page 11)*

5ml/1tsp sugar

175g/6oz whitebait

flour for coating

salt and freshly ground black pepper

oil for deep frying

lemon wedges, to garnish

❚ Roll out the two quantities of dough thinly and cut a 25cm/10-inch equilateral triangle from each. Place the second triangle on top of the first so that a six-pointed star is formed. Gently press the two layers of dough together with your hands.

❚ Heat the olive oil in a frying pan and gently cook the sliced peppers until soft, add the tomato sauce to the pan and stir in the sugar.

❚ When the sauce is warmed through spread it over the star-shaped base and place it in a preheated oven at 240°C/475°F/Gas Mark 9 for 15 minutes.

❚ Thoroughly wash the whitebait under cold running water and pat dry with absorbent kitchen paper.

❚ Season the flour with salt and black pepper and shake the whitebait in it until well coated.

❚ Heat the oil for deep frying. (A good way of testing that it has reached a sufficiently high temperature is to drop in a cube of bread. If the bread turns brown within 60 seconds you can begin frying).

❚ Fry the fish carefully to prevent them sticking together. Arrange the cooked whitebait over the partially cooked base and return the pizza to the oven for a further 5 minutes to finish browning.

❚ Serve garnished with lemon wedges.

TIME: *Preparation takes about 35 minutes. Cooking takes approximately 20 minutes.*

Pizza with Spanish-style Seafood

M A K E S O N E 2 5 C M / 1 0 - I N C H P I Z Z A

This pizza is topped with a mixture of seafood and chicken pieces

INGREDIENTS

30ml/2 tbsp white wine

few strands of saffron

1 quantity Basic Pizza Dough *(page 10)*

1 quantity Tomato Sauce *(page 11)*

45ml/3 tbsp olive oil

1 onion, sliced

1 clove garlic, crushed

1 chicken breast, skinned, boned and sliced

¹/₂ red pepper, seeded and sliced

1 bay leaf

125g/4oz mixed seafood

30ml/2tbsp frozen peas

50g/2oz mozzarella cheese, sliced

▎Put the wine in a small dish, add the saffron and allow to stand for at least 30 minutes.

▎Roll out the pizza dough to form a circle a little larger than 25cm/10 inches in diameter.

▎Place the dough on a lightly oiled baking sheet. Fold over the edges to form a raised border. Allow to stand in a warm place for 15 minutes.

▎Spread the tomato sauce over the base and bake in a preheated oven at 200°C/400°F/Gas Mark 6 for 10 minutes.

▎Meanwhile, heat the oil in a frying pan and fry the onion until beginning to soften.

▎Add the garlic, chicken and red pepper and fry for 2 minutes. Add the wine, saffron and bay leaf and cook for 4 minutes, until the chicken is just cooked.

▎Stir in the seafood and frozen peas.

▎Remove the bay leaf and spoon the mixture over the pizza. Top with mozzarella cheese.

▎Bake in a preheated oven at 200°C/400°F/ Gas Mark 6 for 15–20 minutes or until the base is cooked and golden.

TIME: *Preparation takes about 30 minutes, plus soaking.*

Cooking takes approximately 30 minutes.

Tuna & Prawn Provençal Pizza

MAKES ONE 25CM/10-INCH PIZZA

A *pizza with a fresh Mediterranean flavour*

INGREDIENTS

1 quantity Basic Pizza Dough *(page 10)*

30ml/2tbsp olive oil

1/2 large onion, sliced

1 clove garlic, crushed

1 courgette, thinly sliced

200g/7oz can chopped tomatoes

15ml/1tbsp tomato purée

2.5ml/1/2tsp dried herbes de Provence

salt and freshly ground black pepper

75g/3oz cooked, peeled prawns

175g/6oz can tuna, drained

75g/3oz Saint Paulin cheese, sliced

▌Roll out the pizza dough to form a circle a little larger than 25cm/10 inches in diameter.

▌Place the dough on a lightly oiled baking sheet. Fold over the edges to form a raised border. Allow to stand in a warm place while preparing the topping.

▌Meanwhile, heat the oil in a saucepan and fry the onion for 5 minutes until softened and beginning to brown.

▌Add the garlic and cook for a further minute. Stir in the courgette and fry for 3 minutes.

▌Stir in the tomatoes, tomato purée, herbs and seasoning. Bring to the boil, then reduce the heat and simmer gently for 10–15 minutes.

▌Spread the mixture over the pizza base.

▌Scatter the prawns over the surface of the pizza.

▌Flake the tuna into chunks and arrange on the pizza.

▌Arrange the cheese on top and bake in a preheated oven at 200°C/400°F/Gas Mark 6 for 25–30 minutes or until the base is cooked and golden.

TIME: *Preparation takes about 35 minutes. Cooking takes approximately 30 minutes.*

44

Gravad Lax Pizza

M A K E S   A B O U T   1 6   x   5 C M / 2 - I N C H   P I Z Z A S

These are ideal to serve as canapés before a dinner party with a glass of chilled white wine

INGREDIENTS

50ml/2fl oz white wine vinegar

30ml/2tbsp finely chopped fresh dill

2.5ml/$\frac{1}{2}$tsp sugar

2.5ml/$\frac{1}{2}$tsp salt

freshly ground black pepper

350g/12oz smoked salmon, thinly sliced

1 quantity Quick Pizza Dough *(page 11)*

olive oil

fresh dill sprigs, to garnish

FOR THE SAUCE:

150ml/5fl oz mayonnaise

15ml/1tbsp finely chopped fresh dill

5ml/1tsp prepared English mustard

2.5ml/$\frac{1}{2}$tsp sugar

‖ The day before making these pizzas prepare a marinade using the white wine vinegar, dill, sugar, salt and lots of freshly ground black pepper.

‖ Lay the smoked salmon in a shallow dish and pour over the marinade ensuring that all the fish is coated in the liquid. Cover and leave to stand in the refrigerator for 24 hours.

‖ The following day roll out the pizza dough thinly and cut out 16 5cm/2-inch circles using a plain or fancy cutter. You may need to re-roll the dough.

‖ Place the bases on a lightly oiled baking sheet, prick well with a fork and brush over with a little olive oil. Place in a preheated oven 240°C/475°F/Gas Mark 9 for approximately 10 minutes or until the bases have turned a lightish brown.

‖ Remove them from the oven, transfer to a wire cooling rack and allow to cool completely.

‖ Thoroughly mix together the ingredients for the sauce and spread 5ml/1tsp over each pizza base.

‖ Drain any excess liquid from the smoked salmon and fold or roll each piece and arrange it attractively on top of the pizzas. Garnish each one with a small sprig of fresh dill.

TIME: *Preparation takes about 30 minutes, plus marinating.*

Cooking takes approximately 10 minutes.

45

$\mathscr{P}$izza with $\mathscr{M}$ussels

$\mathscr{S}$eafood is in plentiful supply in Italy, and this delicious pizza is topped with mussels

INGREDIENTS

80g/1½lb mussels

1 quantity Basic Pizza Dough *(page 10)*

280ml/10fl oz stock or water

1 onion, cut into wedges

1 clove garlic, crushed

1 carrot, cut into chunks

1 bouquet garni

few fresh basil leaves

1 quantity Tomato Sauce *(page 11)*

75g/3oz mozzarella cheese, sliced

salt and freshly ground black pepper

olive oil

❚ Prepare the mussels. Scrub well and remove the beards. Discard any that have cracked shells or which do not close when tapped. Place the mussels in a large bowl of cold water and leave for at least 1 hour.

❚ Roll out the pizza dough to form a circle about 25cm/10 inches in diameter.

❚ Place on a lightly oiled baking sheet and prick all over with a fork. Allow to stand in a warm place while preparing the topping.

❚ Put the stock, onion, garlic, carrot and bouquet garni in a large saucepan and bring to the boil. Add the mussels, cover and cook for 5 minutes or until the mussels have opened. Shake the pan or stir frequently during cooking.

❚ Remove the mussels with a slotted spoon and discard any that have not opened.

❚ Remove most of the mussels from the shells, reserving a few in the shells for garnish.

❚ Tear or shred the basil leaves and stir into the tomato sauce along with the mussels.

❚ Spread the tomato mixture over the pizza and arrange the cheese on top. Season with salt and pepper, and drizzle with olive oil.

❚ Bake in a preheated oven at 200°C/400°F/Gas Mark 6 for 25 minutes.

❚ Arrange the mussels in their shells on top of the pizza and return to the oven for 5–10 minutes to heat through. Serve immediately.

TIME: *Preparation takes about 45 minutes, plus soaking.*
Cooking takes approximately 35 minutes.

Pesto & Anchovy Pizza

This pizza combines the very best Italian flavours

INGREDIENTS

1 quantity Basic Pizza Dough *(page 10)*

30ml/2tbsp green pesto sauce

olive oil

12 fresh filleted anchovies, use canned if fresh are unavailable

3 sun-dried tomatoes in oil

175g/6oz mozzarella cheese, grated

salt and freshly ground black pepper

▌Roll out the pizza dough and place it on a lightly oiled pizza pan. Brush the base with olive oil and spread the green pesto over the dough to within an inch of the edge.

▌Sprinkle grated mozzarella over the pesto and arrange the anchovies around the pizza like the spokes of a wheel.

▌Roughly chop the sun-dried tomatoes and scatter them over the pizza and finish with a drizzle of olive oil.

▌Place in a preheated oven 240°C/475°F/Gas Mark 9 for 15–20 minutes until the pizza is golden brown. Serve straightaway with a twist of black pepper.

TIME: *Preparation takes about 15 minutes. Cooking takes approximately 20 minutes.*

Fresh Salmon Pizza

Salmon is no longer a once-in-a-while extravagance

INGREDIENTS

1 quantity Basic Pizza Dough *(page 10)*

1 quantity Tomato Sauce *(page 11)*

2 x 175g/6oz salmon steaks

125g/4oz pitted green olives

15ml/1tbsp snipped chives

olive oil

salt and freshly ground black pepper

▌Roll out the pizza dough and place on a lightly oiled pizza pan. Spread a layer of tomato sauce over the surface leaving an inch of exposed crust around the edge.

▌Place the salmon steaks on a foil-covered grill pan and brush with olive oil and season on both sides. Cook under a preheated grill for 10 minutes on each side until the fish has browned lightly.

▌Skin the salmon, carefully flake the flesh and arrange over the pizza.

▌Scatter over the olives and snipped chives and season.

▌Brush the exposed edge of the pizza with olive oil and place in a preheated oven 240°C/475°F/Gas Mark 9 for 15 minutes or until the pizza has risen well and the edges have turned golden. Serve immediately.

TIME: *Preparation takes about 35 minutes, Cooking takes approximately 15 minutes.*

Peppered Mackerel & Red Onion Pizza

MAKES ONE 30CM/12-INCH PIZZA

One for those who like their pizza a few degrees hotter!

INGREDIENTS

1 quantity Basic Pizza Dough *(page 10)*

1 quantity Tomato Sauce *(page 11)*

125ml/4fl oz olive oil

25ml/1fl oz medium hot chilli sauce

4 peppered mackerel, skinned

dash of Tabasco

2 medium red onions, thinly sliced

Roll out the pizza dough and place on a lightly oiled pizza pan.

Spread tomato sauce over the base to within 2.5cm/1inch of the edge and set to one side.

Make a marinade using 2fl oz/50ml of the olive oil, the chilli sauce and a dash of Tabasco.

Flake the mackerel into bite-sized pieces and place in a shallow bowl, pour over the marinade and gently toss the fish to thoroughly coat.

Heat the remaining olive oil in a frying pan and gently fry the onions until soft.

Arrange the cooked onion over the base, remove the mackerel from the marinade and arrange over the top of the onion.

Brush the edges of the pizza with the remaining marinade and drizzle a couple of teaspoons over the top of the pizza.

Cook in a preheated oven at 240°C/475°F/Gas Mark 9 for 15–20 minutes and serve immediately.

TIME: *Preparation takes about 25 minutes, Cooking takes approximately 20 minutes.*

51

Kids' Fish & Chip Pizza

MAKES ONE FISH-SHAPED PIZZA

Of course, this pizza can be eaten by big kids, too!

INGREDIENTS

1 quantity Basic Pizza Dough *(page 10)*

45ml/3tbsp passata

olive oil

325g/12oz firm white fish such as cod or whiting

225g/8oz small potatoes, cooked

15ml/1tbsp malt vinegar

salt and freshly ground black pepper

52

▌Take three-quarters of the pizza dough and roll it into a circle of roughly 25cm/10 inches in diameter. Using your hands gently stretch it into an oval shape roughly similar to that of a fish's body and lay it on a lightly oiled baking sheet.

▌Shape the remainder of the dough into a tail and attach it to the body by pressing them together firmly.

▌Spread the passata evenly over the pizza leaving a small gap around the edges. Brush the edge with a little olive oil and place in a preheated oven at 240°C/475°F/Gas Mark 9 for 10 minutes.

▌Whilst the base is cooking, skin the fish and cut it into small cubes approximately 1cm/$1/2$inch square and slice the potatoes into 5mm/$1/4$inch thicknesses.

▌Remove the part-cooked pizza from the oven and quickly arrange the potato and fish pieces over the passata. Brush with a little olive oil and sprinkle with malt vinegar.

▌Season well with salt and black pepper and return the pizza to the oven for a further 10 minutes or until the fish is just cooked. Serve immediately.

TIME: *Preparation takes about 20 minutes, Cooking takes approximately 20 minutes.*

Prawn & Pancetta Pizza

MAKES ONE 30CM/12-INCH PIZZA

An appealing mixture of fish and meat in true surf 'n' turf style

INGREDIENTS

1 quantity Basic Pizza Dough *(page 10)*

1 quantity Tomato Sauce *(page 11)*

225g/8oz freshly grated mozzarella cheese

freshly ground black pepper

8 slices of pancetta

175g/6oz cooked peeled prawns

olive oil

oregano leaves, to garnish (optional)

▌Roll out the pizza dough and place it on a lightly oiled pizza pan.

▌Spread the tomato sauce over the base to within 1cm/¹/₂ inch of the edge.

▌Sprinkle half the grated cheese over the pizza and grind over lots of fresh black pepper.

▌Arrange the pancetta slices on top of the cheese and scatter over the prawns.

▌Sprinkle the remaining cheese over the pizza and drizzle some olive oil over the top.

▌Brush the edges of the pizza with olive oil and place in a preheated oven 240°C/475°F/Gas Mark 9 for 15–20 minutes until the base has risen and turned brown and the pancetta is crispy.

▌Garnish the finished pizza with some torn oregano leaves, if liked, and serve immediately.

TIME: *Preparation takes about 10 minutes, Cooking takes approximately 20 minutes.*

53

Pizza Napoletana

MAKES ONE 25CM/10-INCH PIZZA

This is the classic pizza. It originates from Naples

INGREDIENTS

1 quantity Basic Pizza Dough *(page 10)*

6 tomatoes, skinned and sliced

salt and freshly ground black pepper

50g/2oz can anchovy fillets, drained

few fresh basil leaves

75g/3oz mozzarella cheese, sliced

olive oil

▌Roll out to form a circle about 25cm/10 inches in diameter.

▌Place the dough on a lightly oiled baking sheet and prick all over with a fork. Allow to stand in a warm place for 15 minutes.

▌Arrange the tomato slices on top of the pizza base.

▌Season the tomatoes with a little salt and plenty of pepper.

▌Arrange the anchovies on top of the tomatoes, tear the basil leaves into pieces and scatter on top of the pizza.

▌Place the cheese on top and drizzle with a little olive oil.

▌Bake in a preheated oven at 200°C/400°F/Gas Mark 6 for 25–30 minutes or until the base is cooked and golden and the cheese has melted.

TIME: *Preparation takes about 20 minutes, Cooking takes approximately 30 minutes.*

54

Clam Chowder Pizza

MAKES ONE 30CM/12-INCH PIZZA

The fresh, salty smelling clams will soon get your mouth watering

INGREDIENTS

24 fresh clams

1 quantity Basic Pizza Dough *(page 10)*

1 quantity Tomato Sauce *(page 11)*

olive oil

50ml/2fl oz white wine

a few shallots, chopped

chopped fresh parsley, to garnish

❚ If possible, 24 hours prior to making the pizza wash the fresh clams several times in cold water and leave overnight with a sprinkling of flour on the water's surface. The clams will feed on this and pass any dirt or grit from their shells in the process. On the day of use rinse them again in plenty of cold water.

❚ Roll out the pizza dough and place on a lightly oiled pizza pan. Spread the tomato sauce evenly over the dough base and brush the edges with a little olive oil.

❚ Place in a preheated oven 240°C/475°F/Gas Mark 9 and begin cooking for 15–20 minutes.

❚ Meanwhile, in a medium-sized saucepan with a tight-fitting lid, gently heat the white wine and shallots before adding the drained clams and steaming for a couple of minutes.

❚ As soon as the shells have opened remove the pan from the heat to prevent the clams from over-cooking and becoming tough.

❚ Carefully remove the clams from their shells and arrange them over the base just before it has finished cooking. Return the pizza to the oven for a couple of minutes until it is well risen and golden.

❚ Garnish with lots of chopped fresh parsley and serve immediately.

TIME: *Preparation takes about 15 minutes, Cooking takes approximately 20 minutes.*

57

Prawn & Avocado Pizza

MAKES ONE 25CM/10-INCH PIZZA

This delicious blend of seafood and avocado is very refreshing

INGREDIENTS

1 quantity Basic Pizza Dough *(page 10)*

1 quantity Tomato Sauce *(page 11)*

1 ripe avocado

lemon juice

125g/4oz cooked peeled prawns

75g/3oz mozzarella cheese, grated

6 large peeled prawns

▌Roll out the pizza dough to form a circle about 25cm/10 inches in diameter.

▌Place the dough on a lightly oiled baking sheet and prick all over with a fork.

▌Spread the base with the tomato sauce and allow to stand in a warm place while preparing the rest of the topping.

▌Cut the avocado in half and remove the stone. Peel one half and slice, toss in lemon juice and set aside. Peel and chop the other half and toss in lemon juice.

▌Bake the pizza base in a preheated oven at 200°C/400°F/Gas Mark 6 for 10 minutes, then scatter the chopped avocado and peeled prawns over the surface of the pizza.

▌Arrange the sliced avocado on top. Sprinkle with the cheese.

▌Arrange whole prawns on top and bake for 15–20 minutes or until the base is cooked and golden.

TIME: *Preparation takes about 15 minutes. Cooking takes approximately 30 minutes.*

Wild Mushroom Pizza with Two Cheeses

MAKES ONE 25CM/10-INCH PIZZA

Wild mushrooms give a lift to this simple pizza, making it rather special

INGREDIENTS

1 quantity Basic Pizza Dough *(page 10)*

60ml/4 tbsp red pesto sauce

25g/1oz butter

30ml/2tbsp olive oil

1 clove garlic, crushed

50g/2oz shiitake mushrooms, sliced

50g/2oz oyster mushrooms, sliced

50g/2oz brown cap mushrooms, sliced

50g/2oz Brie

50g/2oz goats' cheese

▎ Roll out the pizza dough to form a circle about 25cm/10 inches in diameter.

▎ Place the dough on a lightly oiled baking sheet and prick all over with a fork.

▎ Spread the red pesto over the base and allow to stand in a warm place while preparing the topping.

▎ Melt the butter with the oil and garlic in a large saucepan and sauté the mushrooms for 2–4 minutes, tossing frequently. Scatter the mushrooms over the pizza base.

▎ Remove the rind from the cheese and slice thinly. Arrange on top of the pizza.

▎ Bake in a preheated oven at 200°C/400°F/ Gas Mark 6 for 25–30 minutes or until the base is cooked and golden.

TIME: *Preparation takes about 10 minutes. Cooking takes approximately 35 minutes.*

Sweet Pepper & Sun-dried Tomato Pizza

MAKES ONE 25CM/10-INCH PIZZA

This pizza has a fresh, gutsy flavour and is reminiscent of hot Mediterranean summers

INGREDIENTS

1 red pepper

1 yellow pepper

1 green pepper

olive oil

1 quantity Basic Pizza Dough *(page 10)*

6 sun-dried tomato halves in olive oil, cut into halves
or quarters

few fresh basil leaves

75g/3oz Ricotta cheese

salt and freshly ground black pepper

Cut the peppers in half and remove the stems, cores and seeds. Flatten the peppers with the palm of your hand and brush the skins with olive oil.

Place the peppers skin-side up under a preheated grill. Cook about 5cm/2 inches away from the heat source until the skins are well blistered and charred.

Wrap the peppers in a clean tea towel and leave for 15 minutes. Peel off the charred skins with a small vegetable knife, and slice.

Roll out the pizza dough to form a circle about 25cm/10 inches in diameter.

Place the dough on a lightly oiled baking sheet and prick all over with a fork. Allow to stand in a warm place for 15 minutes.

Scatter the sliced peppers randomly over the pizza base. Arrange the sun-dried tomatoes on top.

Tear the basil leaves and scatter over the pizza. Place teaspoonsful of cheese over the pizza and season well.

Drizzle with olive oil and bake in a preheated oven at 200°C/400°F/Gas Mark 6 for 25–30 minutes or until the base is cooked and golden.

TIME: *Preparation takes about 30 minutes.*
Cooking takes approximately 30 minutes.

60

Goats' Cheese & Devilled Nut Pizza

MAKES ONE 30CM/12-INCH PIZZA

An appealing mix of soft cheese and spicy, crunchy nuts

INGREDIENTS

1 quantity Quick Pizza Dough *(page 11)*

45ml/3tbsp passata or Tomato Sauce *(page 11)*

175g/6oz crumbly goats' cheese

freshly ground black pepper

25g/1oz unsalted cashew nuts, halved

25g/1oz pine nuts

5ml/1tsp cayenne pepper

5ml/1tsp English mustard powder

olive oil

▌Roll out the pizza dough and place on a lightly oiled pizza pan.

▌Spread a thin layer of passata or tomato sauce over the pizza to within 2.5cm/1inch of the edge.

▌Crumble the goats' cheese quite finely and sprinkle over the top of the tomato sauce. Season with plenty of black pepper.

▌Place the cashew nuts, pine nuts, cayenne pepper and mustard powder into a clean freezer bag or similar and shake vigorously so the nuts become lightly coated in the spices.

▌Empty the contents of the bag into a sieve and shake to remove the excess spices before scattering the devilled nuts over the top of the pizza.

▌Drizzle a little olive oil over the pizza and place in a preheated oven 240°C/475°F/Gas Mark 9 for 20 minutes until the pizza is well risen and golden brown. Serve immediately.

TIME: *Preparation takes about 15 minutes.*
Cooking takes approximately 20 minutes.

61

Spicy Vegetarian Pizza

MAKES ONE 25CM/10-INCH PIZZA

A *wholesome vegetarian pizza, very rich in flavour*

INGREDIENTS

1 quantity Basic Pizza Dough (*page 10*)

60ml/4tbsp olive oil

1 large onion, chopped

2 cloves garlic, crushed

1 red chilli, seeded and chopped

1 green chilli, seeded and chopped

400g/14oz can chopped tomatoes

dash of Tabasco

1/2 red pepper, seeded

1/2 green pepper, seeded

1/2 yellow pepper, seeded

75g/3oz mushrooms, sliced

chopped fresh marjoram or 2.5ml/1/2tsp dried marjoram

50g/2oz Cheddar cheese, grated

50g/2oz Red Leicester cheese, grated

Roll out the pizza dough to form a circle about 25cm/10 inches in diameter.

Place the dough on a lightly oiled baking sheet and prick all over with a fork. Allow to stand in a warm place while preparing the topping.

Heat 30ml/2tbsp of the oil in a saucepan and fry the onion, garlic and chillies for about 5 minutes or until softened.

Stir in the tomatoes and Tabasco and bring to the boil, then reduce the heat and simmer gently for 15 minutes.

Meanwhile, slice 1 or 2 rings from the peppers and set aside. Chop the remaining peppers.

Heat the remaining oil in a frying pan and fry the chopped peppers for 2 minutes. Add the mushrooms and continue to cook for 3 minutes.

Spread the tomato sauce over the pizza base and cover with the sautéed peppers and mushrooms.

Mix together the marjoram and cheeses and sprinkle over the pizza.

Top with the reserved pepper rings and brush the rings with a little extra oil.

Bake in a preheated oven at 200°C/400°F/Gas Mark 6 for 25–30 minutes or until the base is cooked and golden.

TIME: *Preparation takes about 35 minutes. Cooking takes approximately 30 minutes.*

63

Fried Pizza

This *method of cooking is popular in many Italian households*

INGREDIENTS

175g/6oz plain flour

2.5ml/½tsp baking powder

pinch of salt

25g/1oz butter

90ml/6 tbsp milk

olive oil, for shallow frying

3 tomatoes, skinned and chopped

5ml/1tsp capers

5ml/1tsp chopped fresh oregano or

2.5ml/½tsp dried oregano

50g/2oz mozzarella cheese, grated

‖ Sift the flour, baking powder and salt into a mixing bowl. Rub in the butter until the mixture resembles fine breadcrumbs. Mix in enough milk to form a soft dough.

‖ Roll out the dough to form a 20cm/8-inch round.

‖ Heat enough oil to coat a heavy-based frying pan, then cover the base with the dough. Cook over a low heat for 5 minutes or until the underside is golden.

‖ Carefully turn the pizza base over. Scatter the chopped tomatoes, capers and oregano on top of the pizza and cook for 3 minutes.

‖ Sprinkle with the cheese, cover with a lid or plate and cook for another 3 minutes or until the cheese melts.

TIME: *Preparation takes about 10 minutes.*
Cooking takes approximately 10 minutes.

Bubble & Squeak Pizza

A *perfect way of using up leftovers*

INGREDIENTS

1 quantity Basic Pizza Dough *(page 10)*

225g/8oz mashed potato

125g/4oz cooked vegetables such as sprouts or parsnips

50ml/2fl oz tomato ketchup

50g/2oz can anchovy fillets, drained and roughly chopped

salt and freshly ground black pepper

50g/2oz freshly grated Parmesan cheese

olive oil

‖ Divide the pizza dough in two and roll each half into a 20cm/8-inch circle. Place on a lightly oiled pizza tin.

‖ In a large mixing bowl roughly mash together the potatoes and vegetables.

‖ Beat in the tomato ketchup and chopped anchovies until both are well combined, then season well.

‖ Brush the surface of the dough base with a little olive oil then spoon on the topping. Use a fork to spread the bubble and squeak evenly over the pizza.

‖ Sprinkle the grated Parmesan over the top and finish with a good twist of pepper and a drizzle of olive oil.

‖ Place in a preheated oven 240°C/475°F/Gas Mark 9 for 20 minutes or until the cheese has melted.

TIME: *Preparation takes about 15 minutes.*
Cooking takes approximately 20 minutes.

Herb Bread with Tomatoes & Olive Oil

SERVES 4

This is a perfect dish for a light summer lunch

INGREDIENTS

1 large French stick

30ml/2tbsp finely chopped fresh mixed herbs such as
basil, mint and parsley

125g/4oz unsalted butter, softened

175g/6oz mozzarella cheese, thinly sliced

6 ripe plum tomatoes, sliced

freshly ground black pepper

olive oil

pitted black olives

fresh basil leaves, to garnish

▌Slice the French stick into 2.5cm/1-inch thick rounds and arrange them on an attractive heat-resistant pan.

▌Beat the chopped fresh herbs into the softened butter and spread a small amount over each slice of bread. Be sparing with the butter or the bread will become soggy.

▌Place the pan under a preheated grill and leave until the butter has melted into the bread and the surface has browned lightly.

▌Turn the slices of French bread over and repeat the process. When the second side has browned remove the slices of bread from the grill.

▌Place a slice of mozzarella cheese onto each piece and top with a slice of tomato. Grind over lots of fresh black pepper, drizzle plenty of olive oil and scatter the black olives over the toast. Do not worry if the oil runs onto the dish as this can be mopped up with the bread when eating.

▌Return to the grill for a further 2–3 minutes until the cheese has softened. Remove and finish by garnishing with some roughly torn basil leaves. Serve straightaway with plenty of chilled white wine.

TIME: *Preparation takes about 15 minutes.
Cooking takes approximately 5 minutes.*

Banana Pizza

MAKES ONE 25CM/10-INCH PIZZA

A *super sweet pizza that is best eaten hot and*
fresh. It does not reheat well

INGREDIENTS

1 quantity Basic Pizza Dough *(page 10)*

6 large bananas, sliced and tossed in lemon juice

75g/3oz light muscovado sugar

whipped cream, to serve

Roll out the pizza dough to form a circle a little larger
than 25cm/10 inches in diameter.

Place the dough on a lightly oiled baking sheet. Fold
over the edges to form a raised border. Allow to stand in
a warm place for 15 minutes.

Arrange the sliced banana on top of the pizza.

Sprinkle with the sugar and bake in a preheated oven at
200°C/400°F/Gas Mark 6 for 25–30 minutes or until
the base is cooked and golden. Allow to cool slightly
before serving accompanied with freshly whipped
cream.

TIME: *Preparation takes about 15 minutes.*
Cooking takes approximately 30 minutes.

Mushroom Pizza

MAKES ONE 23CM/9-INCH PIZZA

F*resh tomato sauce, oregano and*
mushrooms bring a taste of summer

INGREDIENTS

1 quantity Quick Pizza Dough *(page 11)*

30ml/2tbsp olive oil

125g/4oz mushrooms

chopped fresh oregano

salt and freshly ground black pepper

1 clove garlic, cut in half

1 quantity Tomato Sauce *(page 11)*

75g/3oz mozzarella cheese, grated

30ml/2tbsp freshly grated Parmesan cheese

Roll out the pizza dough to form a circle about
23cm/9 inches in diameter. Place the dough on a lightly
oiled baking sheet and prick all over with a fork.

Bake in a preheated oven at 200°C/400°F/Gas Mark 6
for 15 minutes or until golden. Reduce the heat to
180°C/350°F/Gas Mark 4.

Heat the oil in a small pan and fry the mushrooms until
soft. Stir in the oregano and season with salt and pepper.

Rub the pizza base with the cut edge of the garlic.
Spread with the tomato sauce.

Arrange the mushrooms on top. Sprinkle mozzarella,
then Parmesan, over the mushrooms.

Return to the oven and bake for 10–15 minutes or
until the cheese melts.

TIME: *Preparation takes about 15 minutes.*
Cooking takes approximately 30 minutes.

69

Roast Aubergine & Tomato Pizza

MAKES ONE 25CM/10-INCH PIZZA

This mouthwatering pizza is perfect for cold nights by the fire

INGREDIENTS

1 large aubergine

salt

1 quantity Basic Pizza Dough *(page 10)*

90ml/6tbsp passata

olive oil

2 beef tomatoes, sliced

2 cloves garlic, sliced

freshly ground black pepper

fresh basil leaves

70

Thickly slice the aubergine and spread out on a plate. Sprinkle liberally with salt and leave to stand for 20 minutes.

Roll out the pizza dough to form a circle about 25cm/10 inches in diameter.

Place the dough on a lightly oiled baking sheet and prick all over with a fork.

Spread the base with the passata. Allow to stand in a warm place while preparing the topping.

Rinse the aubergine and pat dry. Heat about 60ml/4 tbsp olive oil in a large frying pan and fry the aubergine slices on both sides until beginning to brown. You may need to do this in batches; add extra olive oil as required.

Arrange alternate slices of aubergine and tomato on top of the pizza.

Sprinkle with garlic and season well. Tear the basil into pieces and scatter on top.

Drizzle with olive oil and bake in a preheated oven at 200°C/400°F/Gas Mark 6 for 25–30 minutes or until the base is cooked and golden.

TIME: *Preparation takes about 20 minutes, plus standing.*

Cooking takes approximately 40 minutes.

VARIATION: *Top with any cheese of your choice.*

Pizza with Four Cheeses

MAKES ONE 28CM/11-INCH PIZZA

A *pizza for cheese fans, this recipe uses four Italian varieties*

INGREDIENTS

1 quantity Basic Pizza Dough *(page 10)*

1 quantity Tomato Sauce *(page 11)*

3 plum tomatoes, sliced

50g/2oz Gorgonzola cheese, cut into small chunks

50g/2oz mozzarella cheese, sliced

50g/2oz Fontina or Bel Paese cheese, sliced or cut into small chunks

50g/2oz Dolcelatte cheese, crumbled

few fresh marjoram leaves, to garnish

Roll out the pizza dough to form a circle about 28cm/11 inches in diameter.

Place the dough on a lightly oiled baking sheet. Fold over the edges to form a raised border.

Spread with the tomato sauce and allow to stand in a warm place for 10–15 minutes.

Arrange the sliced tomato on top of the base and bake in a preheated oven at 200°C/400°F/Gas Mark 6 for 10 minutes.

Remove the partially cooked base from the oven and arrange each cheese over a quarter of the pizza.

Return to the oven for 15–20 minutes or until the base is cooked and golden and the cheese has melted.

Serve sprinkled with a few fresh marjoram leaves.

TIME: *Preparation takes about 20 minutes. Cooking takes approximately 30 minutes.*

Potato & Onion Pizza

MAKES ONE 25CM/10-INCH PIZZA

A *traditional-style pizza which is ideal for parties or picnics*

INGREDIENTS

1 quantity Basic Pizza Dough (*page 10*)

olive oil

350g/12oz small potatoes, peeled

2 onions, thinly sliced

salt and freshly ground black pepper

3 cloves garlic, sliced

small sprigs of fresh rosemary or

15ml/1tbsp dried rosemary

Roll out the pizza dough to form a rectangle about 28 x 18cm/11 x 7 inches.

Place the dough on a lightly oiled baking sheet and prick all over with a fork.

Brush the base liberally with olive oil and allow to stand in a warm place while preparing the topping.

Cook the potatoes in boiling water for 5 minutes, drain and slice thinly.

Arrange the onions over the base of the pizza and season well.

Arrange the potato slices over the onion and scatter with the garlic. Dot with sprigs of fresh rosemary or scatter with dried rosemary.

Drizzle olive oil all over the pizza then bake in a preheated oven at 220°C/425°F/Gas Mark 7 for 15 minutes.

Reduce the heat to 190°C/375°F/Gas Mark 5 and continue to cook for 25 minutes or until golden all over.

If the potatoes have not browned sufficiently, place under a preheated grill for a few minutes.

TIME: *Preparation takes about 20 minutes. Cooking takes approximately 40 minutes.*

Courgette & Garlic Pizza

MAKES ONE 30CM/12-INCH PIZZA

The courgettes absorb the garlic to make a really tasty pizza

INGREDIENTS

1 quantity Basic Pizza Dough *(page 10)*

½ quantity Tomato Sauce *(page 11)*

60ml/4tbsp olive oil

4 cloves garlic, roughly chopped

4 small courgettes

5ml/1tsp dried or fresh chopped oregano

salt and freshly ground black pepper

50g/2oz Parmesan cheese, grated

▌Roll out the pizza dough and place it on a lightly oiled pizza pan.

▌Spread the tomato sauce thinly over the dough to within 2.5cm/1 inch of the edge and set the pizza to one side.

▌Heat 45ml/3 tbsp of the olive oil in a frying pan, and add the garlic.

▌Slice the courgettes into 5mm/¼ inch slices. When the garlic has coloured a little, add them to the pan along with the oregano.

▌Fry the courgettes gently until they are lightly browned on both sides, adding a little more olive oil if necessary.

▌Using a slotted spoon, carefully remove the courgettes and garlic and arrange them over the pizza base. Season the pizza well with salt and pepper and sprinkle over the grated Parmesan cheese.

▌Brush the edges of the pizza with the remaining olive oil and place in a preheated oven 240°C/475°F/Gas Mark 9 for 20 minutes or until the dough has risen and turned golden and the cheese has melted. Serve immediately.

TIME: *Preparation takes about 15 minutes.*
Cooking takes approximately 20 minutes.

*I*ndex

76